Native American Biographies

SEQUOYAH

Anne M. Todd

Heinemann Library
Chicago, Illinois

© 2004 Heinemann Library
a division of Reed Elsevier Inc.
Chicago, Illinois

Customer Service   888–454–2279

Visit our website at www.heinemannlibrary.com

Designed by Kim Saar/Heinemann Library
Maps by John Fleck
Photo research by Alan Gottlieb
Printed in China by WKT Company Limited

08 07 06 05 04
10 9 8 7 6 5 4 3 2 1

Library of Congress Cataloging-in-Publication Data
Todd, Anne M.
  Sequoyah / Anne M. Todd.
    p. cm. -- (Native American biographies)
  Summary: A biography of Sequoyah, a member of the Cherokee tribe who was responsible for creating a syllabary that put the Cherokee language in writing, describing his childhood, work as a blacksmith, and service for the British in the War of 1812.
  Includes bibliographical references and index.
  ISBN 1-4034-5005-6 (lib. bdg.) -- ISBN 1-4034-5012-9 (pbk.)
  1. Sequoyah, 1770?-1843--Juvenile literature. 2. Cherokee Indians--Biography--Juvenile literature. 3. Cherokee language--Alphabet--Juvenile literature. 4. Cherokee language--Writing--Juvenile literature. 5. United States--History--War of 1812--Juvenile literature. [1. Sequoyah, 1770?-1843. 2. Cherokee Indians--Biography. 3. Indians of North America--Biography.] I. Title. II. Series: Native American biographies (Heinemann Library (Firm))
  E99.C5S36 2004
  975.004'97557'0092--dc22
                            2003020493

Acknowledgments
The author and publisher are grateful to the following for permission to reproduce copyright material:
p. 4 Raymond Gehman/Corbis; p. 7 Jay Dickman/Corbis; p. 8 Lisa LaRue/Cherokee Nation Cultural Resource Center; p. 10 Marilyn "Angel" Wynn/NativeStock.com; pp. 11, 22 Gilcrease Museum; p. 12 Library of Congress/Neg. #LC-USZ62-46199; p. 13 New Echota Historic Site; pp. 14, 15 Frank H. McClung Museum/University of Tennessee; p. 17 Eastern National, photo by Ed Elvidge; p. 18 Courtesy Department of Library Services, American Museum of Natural History/Neg#323618; p. 20 National Portrait Gallery, Smithsonian Institution/Art Resource, NY; p. 23 Library of Congress/Neg. #LC-USZ62-115659; p. 25 Murv Jacob/Tahlequah, Oklahoma; p. 26 Library of Congress/Neg. #LC-USZ62-61141; p. 28 Robert Holmes/Corbis; p. 29 Annie Griffiths Belt/Corbis

Cover photographs by (foreground) Rare Books and Manuscripts Division/New York Public Library/Astor, Lenox and Tilden Foundations, (background) Alex Brandon/Heinemann Library

Special thanks to Lisa LaRue for her help in the preparation of this book.

The image of Sequoyah on the cover of this book was painted in the middle 1800s.
The background shows a river in the eastern United States.

Contents

Some words are shown in bold, **like this.** You can find out what they mean by looking in the glossary.

Sequoyah Teaches the Cherokees

Sequoyah and his six-year-old daughter, Ahyokah, had a big job to do. They needed to teach people how to read and write their **tribe's** language. Until now, the Cherokees' language had only been spoken. Sequoyah had created a **syllabary** that would allow Cherokees to read and write in their own language.

This display at the Sequoyah Birthplace Museum in Vonore, Tennessee, shows Sequoyah with Ahyokah.

4

A large group of people gathered. Sequoyah told Ahyokah to stand far away from the crowd. Then Sequoyah asked someone in the audience to speak. Sequoyah wrote down what he heard on a piece of paper. He signaled for Ahyokah to return. Sequoyah handed the paper to her. Ahyokah read aloud the syllables on the paper. It was exactly as what the audience member had told Sequoyah. Sequoyah's syllabary really worked!

In 1980 the United States Postal Service made a Sequoyah postage stamp.

USA
19c

Sequoyah

Growing Up Cherokee

Sequoyah was born around 1776 in Taskigi, Tennessee. His mother was Cherokee and his father was white. Sequoyah's mother, Wuh-teh, belonged to the Cherokee Paint **Clan**. Sequoyah's father was probably a trader named Nathaniel Gist. He left the family when Sequoyah was still a baby. Sequoyah never knew him.

Cherokee Clans

Cherokees are always born into their mother's clan. Today there are seven Cherokee clans: Bird, Blue, Deer, Long Hair, Paint, Wild Potato, and Wolf.

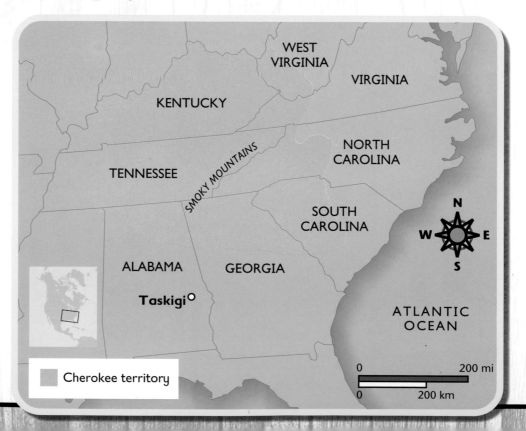

WEST VIRGINIA

VIRGINIA

KENTUCKY

NORTH CAROLINA

TENNESSEE

SMOKY MOUNTAINS

SOUTH CAROLINA

N
W E
S

ALABAMA

GEORGIA

Taskigi

ATLANTIC OCEAN

Cherokee territory

0   200 mi
0   200 km

Sequoyah did not have any brothers or sisters. He and his mother lived on a small dairy farm. He helped his mother take care of the cows. He also helped make cheese. On cold winter nights, Sequoyah and the other children listened to **elders** tell stories around a fire.

Sequoyah grew up in the Smoky Mountains in the eastern part of present-day Tennessee.

When Sequoyah was young, his mother and relatives noticed that he had a problem with one of his legs. It may have gotten hurt because of a sickness or during a hunting trip. Sequoyah walked with a **limp** for the rest of his life.

These Cherokee children are enjoying a story told by storyteller Choogie Kingfisher.

Sequoyah was a shy boy. His leg made it hard for him to run and play with the other boys. Most Cherokee boys spent a lot of time playing games and sports. Sequoyah usually just watched these games because of the problem with his leg.

Cherokee Stories

Sequoyah liked to listen to **tribal elders** tell Cherokee stories. Elders told stories about how the Cherokee people came to be on Earth, important Cherokee events of long ago, and funny stories about **trickster** animals.

Cherokee children learn from their relatives. **Elders** taught Sequoyah about Cherokee history. Sequoyah also learned to ride a horse. His uncles taught him to use a **blowgun** to hunt squirrels, birds, and other small animals. When he got older, Sequoyah went hunting with his uncles.

Blowguns

A blowgun is made from a hollow plant called river cane. Cherokees load the hollow plant with sharp thistles. They aim the blowgun and blow the thistle at their target.

3 1833 04697 7960

Today some Cherokee men compete at using the blowgun.

This drawing was made by Sequoyah when he was an adult.

Sequoyah spent a lot of time by himself. He enjoyed sitting in the woods and drawing what he saw. He also liked to make wood furniture. Sequoyah built a shed for the milk and cream that his mother got from her dairy cows.

Settlers built homes on Cherokee land during the 1770s.

When Sequoyah was still a young boy, **settlers** came into Cherokee territory. The settlers fought to take the land away from the Cherokees. They wanted to build houses and use the land to grow crops. The Cherokees had to fight to keep their land.

Timeline

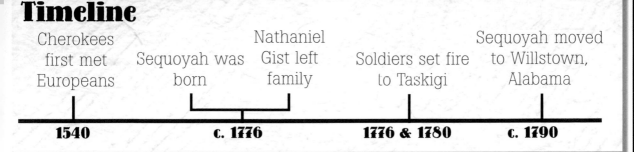

Cherokees first met Europeans	Sequoyah was born	Nathaniel Gist left family	Soldiers set fire to Taskigi	Sequoyah moved to Willstown, Alabama
1540	**c. 1776**		**1776 & 1780**	**c. 1790**

In 1776 the settlers set fire to Sequoyah's hometown, Taskigi, in present-day Tennessee. Sequoyah and his mother, along with other Cherokee families, went to the mountains for safety. They lived there for several years. The settlers set fire to Taskigi again in 1780. Around this time many Cherokees moved to Willstown, Alabama. They could start a new life there. Sequoyah and his mother went, too.

This is what the Cherokee town of New Echota might have look like in Sequoyah's time.

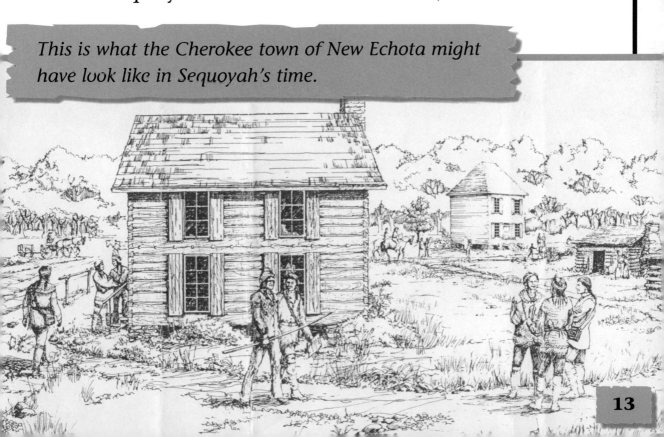

Change for Sequoyah

Sequoyah and his mother opened a trading company in Willstown. They sold knives, beads, **fabric**, and other **goods** in their store. People traded animal furs for the goods. Sequoyah and his mother used the furs to buy more goods. When Sequoyah's mother died, Sequoyah ran the store.

*Many eastern American Indian **tribes** traded furs and other goods with **settlers**.*

The Cherokees loved beautiful silver jewelry pieces like this one.

Sequoyah also taught himself to make jewelry. He melted down silver coins and shaped them into necklaces and earrings. People loved Sequoyah's work. Around this time, Sequoyah met and married a woman named Utiyu. They started a family. Sequoyah taught himself a new skill. He became a **blacksmith.** As a blacksmith, Sequoyah made and repaired tools, such as hoes and axes. Sequoyah was a good blacksmith and had many customers.

Sequoyah had seen how **settlers** wrote words in English on paper. Sequoyah called this paper "talking leaves." Sequoyah wanted Cherokees to be able to read and write in their own language, too. He decided to create a way to write the Cherokee language.

War of 1812

For many years after the **American Revolution,** Great Britain did not let the United States trade overseas. As a result, the two countries went to war. This was called the War of 1812. After the war, Great Britain and the United States were on friendlier terms.

Timeline

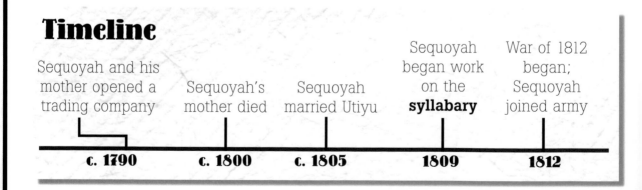

Sequoyah and his mother opened a trading company	Sequoyah's mother died	Sequoyah married Utiyu	Sequoyah began work on the **syllabary**	War of 1812 began; Sequoyah joined army
c. 1790	c. 1800	c. 1805	1809	1812

Sequoyah fought in the Battle of Horseshoe Bend during the War of 1812.

But first Sequoyah took time to serve his country. In 1812 the United States and Great Britain fought in a war. Some Cherokees, like Sequoyah, joined the United States Army. Sequoyah fought for the United States. Then he returned home to continue his work as a **blacksmith.**

Sequoyah's Syllabary

After a while, Sequoyah stopped working at his **blacksmith** shop. He spent all his time working on a written form of the Cherokee language. He decided not to use an alphabet, which is what the English language uses. Instead he would use a **syllabary.** He spent years listening to the Cherokee language, trying to figure out what sounds he heard.

Sequoyah worked for twelve years to create his syllabary.

18

Many people thought Sequoyah had gone crazy. He spent long hours alone with his work. Utiyu did not understand Sequoyah's **passion** for creating a written language. They got a divorce. He later met and married a woman named Sally Waters.

In Their Own Words

Sequoyah's friends told him that he would no longer be respected if he continued to work on the syllabary. Sequoyah responded by saying: "It is not our people that have advised me to this. . . It is not therefore our people who can be blamed if I am wrong."

Sequoyah identified 200 sounds in the Cherokee language. He created a **symbol** to represent each sound. He knew that it would be hard for most people to remember 200 symbols. From 1818 to 1821, Sequoyah worked to make a **syllabary** with fewer symbols. He ended up with 86 symbols.

Syllabary or Alphabet?

An alphabet is a set of letters. Different letters put together in different ways create different sounds. A syllabary is a set of symbols, each representing a different sound. For example, *banana* has six letters. Using a syllabary, *banana* has only three symbols—one for the sound "buh," another for "nah," and a third for "nuh."

At last, Sequoyah had created a written language. To test his syllabary, he taught his family to read and write in Cherokee. It worked! They learned the syllabary easily and could **communicate** through writing. Sequoyah and his daughter Ahyokah traveled together teaching Sequoyah's syllabary to groups of Cherokees.

Sequoyah proudly holds his completed syllabary.

Until 1821 the Cherokee people had recorded their history by telling stories. These stories passed from one generation to the next. But now they had a way to write down their history. They could **communicate** with friends and family who lived far away. They could keep records at **council** meetings. The Cherokee people no longer thought Sequoyah was crazy. They now thought he was a genius.

In 1828 the first *Cherokee Phoenix* came out. It was a newspaper

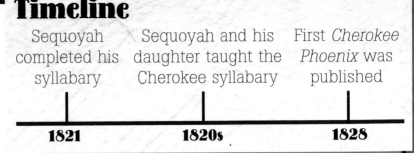

Timeline

Sequoyah completed his syllabary	Sequoyah and his daughter taught the Cherokee syllabary	First *Cherokee Phoenix* was published
1821	1820s	1828

written in both Cherokee and English. Thanks to Sequoyah's **syllabary**, the Cherokee language was in print for the first time ever. The Cherokee people honored Sequoyah with a silver medal. He wore the medal throughout the rest of his life.

First Newspaper

Samuel Austin Worcester helped publish the *Cherokee Phoenix*. It was the first newspaper to print articles in an American Indian language.

This is the front page of the Cherokee Phoenix *from 1828.*

23

Uniting the Cherokees

All was not well within the Cherokee **Nation.** In 1828 some Cherokees, including Sequoyah, signed a **treaty** with the United States government. The government promised Cherokees money and supplies if they would move to present-day Arkansas. The treaty also promised that the Cherokees would never have to move again. But they did. In 1838 the Cherokee were forced to move even further west, into present-day Oklahoma.

Sequoyah and his family moved into a small log house. At home, they raised livestock. Sequoyah became a teacher. He taught his students how to use the **syllabary**. He also told stories about the old Cherokee way of life.

*About 4,000 Cherokees died from sickness, **exhaustion,** or cold because of their journey to Oklahoma.*

Trail of Tears

Some Cherokees did not sign the 1828 treaty. In 1838 the United States forced these Cherokees to move. 16,000 Cherokees had to walk 800 miles (1,287 kilometers) to present-day Oklahoma. This was the Trail of Tears.

25

In 1842, when Sequoyah was about 70 years old, he decided to travel to Mexico. When he was a boy, his mother told him that a group of Cherokees had once moved to Mexico. Sequoyah wanted to see this place and meet the Cherokees living there. He went with his son and some other men.

*The Cherokee people wrote their own **constitution** in 1839. This kept their government separate from the government of the United States.*

In Their Own Words

"The old and the young find no difficulty in learning to read and write in their native language. . . [They can write letters to] their distant friends with the same facility as the whites do."

—Cherokee chief John Ross

Within a year after he left for Mexico, Sequoyah died near a small Mexican village. The entire Cherokee **Nation** and all of the United States mourned the loss of a great man.

Cherokees Today

Today the United States government recognizes three Cherokee groups. Members of the Cherokee Nation and the United Keetoowah Band of Cherokee Indians live in Oklahoma. The Eastern Band of Cherokee Indians is in North Carolina.

Timeline

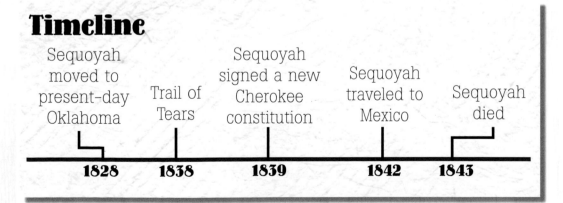

Sequoyah moved to present-day Oklahoma	Trail of Tears	Sequoyah signed a new Cherokee constitution	Sequoyah traveled to Mexico	Sequoyah died
1828	1838	1839	1842	1843

Sequoyah Remembered Today

Sequoyah is still remembered today. The sequoia tree, which can be found in California, is named after him. Sequoias can grow to be the tallest trees in the United States. The Sequoia National Park and the Sequoia National Forest are both in California. They were named to honor Sequoyah.

In Their Own Words

One former member of Congress, Sam Houston, said: "Your invention of the [syllabary] is worth more to your people than two bags full of gold in the hands of every Cherokee."

This sign is located in the Sequoia National Park.

erokee Translation

$150	CONES, ᎣᏍᏗ-ᎣᎨᎥ ᏍᏗᎢᎢ		35 45 55	
175	CHOCOLATE DIP CONES, ᎠᎣᏚᏇ ᎣᎣᎠᎠᏟ ᏍᏗᎢᎢ		50 60	
100	FLOATS ᎣᎤᎩᏟ ᎠᎢᏟᎣᎤᎢ		55 75	
120	FREEZES ᎣᏁᎣᎤᎢ ᎳᎢᎢ		75	
120	BANANA SPLITS, ᎢᎡᎡ ᎠᎣᎤ Ꭽ ᏴᎢ		160	
140	MALTS and SHAKES, ᎣᎣᎢ ᎠᏚ ᎣᏟᏂᏟ		75	
140	SUNDAES, ᎠᎦ ᏇᎡ ᎠᎦᏴ ᏴᏟᎢ		60 75	
140	Chocolate, Cherry, Butterscotch, Strawberry and Pineapple			
160	SUNDAES, Hot Fudge, Butter Pecan		70 85	
160	DRINKS, ᎣᏴᏟ ᏟᎢᏟᎣᎤᎢ			
140	COKE, ROOT BEER, Dr.PEPPER, SPRITE 2		40 55 75	
85	ORANGE or GRAPE SLUSH, ᏚᏟᎦᎣᎤᏟᎣᎢ		40 55 75	
70	LIMEADE or LEMONADE, ᏟᏅᏂᏍ ᏚᏟᎦᎣᎤᏟᎣᎢ		55 75	
85	ICE TEA, ᎣᎢᏟᎩ ᎠᏚᎣᎢ		40 55 75	
100	COFFEE, ᎡᎡ		25	
70				
70	We Use "BUNNY" Bread and Buns			
85	"hous" ᎠᎩᎢᎠ 55 ᎣᏂ ᎦᎤ ᏄᏟ			

Public schools within the Cherokee **Nation** use Sequoyah's **syllabary** to teach Cherokee. College students can learn Cherokee at Northeastern State University in Tahlequah, Oklahoma. Students everywhere also learn about Sequoyah's life. His gift to the Cherokee people was the written word.

Glossary

American Revolution war that the American colonies fought to gain independence from Great Britain (1775–1783)

blacksmith person who makes things from iron

blowgun weapon made from river cane that was used to hunt small animals

clan group of people who are related

communicate pass ideas between people

constitution plan for government

council group of leaders who make decisions for a group of people

elder older person, such as a grandparent, who is treated with respect

exhaustion being extremely tired

fabric cloth

goods something made to sell

limp favoring one leg while walking

nation   group of American Indians of the
  same tribe

passion   strong feeling about something

settler   person who makes a home in a
  new place

syllabary   set of letter groups. In Sequoyah's
  Cherokee syllabary, each group of letters
  represents a sound or group of sounds.

symbol   something that stands for something else

treaty   agreement between governments or
  groups of people

tribe   group of people who share language,
  customs, beliefs, and often government

trickster   sneaky character that appears in
  various kinds of stories

More Books to Read

Fitterer, C. Ann. *Sequoyah: Native American Scholar*. Eden Prairie, Minn.: The Child's World, 2002.

Shaughnessy, Diane. *Sequoyah: Inventor of the Cherokee Written Language*. New York: Rosen Publishing Group, 1998.

Williams, Suzanne Morgan. *Cherokee Indians*. Chicago: Heinemann Library, 2003.

Index